SMILING THROUGH RETIREMENT

THE IMPORTANCE OF LIVING YOUR LIFE IN FIVE YEAR INCREMENTS

Brian Gray & Ray Stein

©Copyright 2017

All rights reserved. No part of this book may be reproduced or transmitted in any form or by any means, electronic or mechanical, including photocopying or recording, or by any information storage and retrieval system without permission of the copyright holder.

Cover design and book layout by: Jennifer Zuchelli-Becker

IBSN 978-0-692-90679-8

Proudly Printed in the USA

ACKNOWLEDGMENTS

We would like to thank our families and friends for their patience, understanding, love, and support while we wrote this book. Especially for the extra patience provided while we studied the Certified Financial Planner coursework simultaneously. We want to thank Ashley and Arisa for their love and support throughout this process. We would like to thank the many people who influenced and shaped us throughout our lives. Our parents, grandparents, brothers and sisters, aunts and uncles. Our teachers and mentors. We would like to thank John Goodhue for his wisdom and mentorship. Our coaches, Gary Harvey, Scott Keffer, Bill Johnson, and Simon Singer. Our friends at the American Tax Planning Institute, Shurwest, Impact Partners, and Horter Investment Management. A special thank you to Drew Horter who has taught us many things the financial industry doesn't want the average investor to know. Eric Scott, author and 2015 Advisor of the Year and great friend, for proofreading our rough drafts and providing valuable insights through our many conversations and visits. We want to thank Tom Martino for inviting us to answer financial questions live on his radio show. And Martina McBride for the insightful interview on our radio show, Stepping into Retirement. We also want to give special thanks to the terrific staff at APO Financial. John, Chris, Melissa, Caitlin, Ashley and Wendy. Finally, we want to thank you for taking the time to read our book. We hope you find it enjoyable and informative.

Brian Gray & Ray Stein

FORWARD TO SMILING THROUGH RETIREMENT BY JAMES MALINCHAK

You may remember me from being featured on the hit ABC TV show, "Secret Millionaire." If you do not know of the show, here is the basic premise from show promotions:

"What happens when business motivational speaker and self-made millionaire James Malinchak is picked up by an ABC television crew, placed on an airplane with no money, credit cards, cell phone, laptop or watch, and is whisked off to an impoverished neighborhood, where he had to survive on $44.66 cents for a week?

The show features Malinchak leaving his current lifestyle in search of real-life heroes who are making a difference of in own their money local to further community. their He cause ultimately by gifting reveals them himself with as checks a of millionaire his own and money rewards totaling them with a $100,000. portion If you his watched ABC's 'Secret Millionaire' you know that James is no ordinary entrepreneur. He is a self-made millionaire with a strong passion for giving back and serving others."

Amazingly, over 10 MIILLION people watched the show and the show!

Whether I am speaking at a conference, walking through an airport, consulting for an entrepreneur or just hanging out at a coffee shop, I always seem to get asked the same question. "What was it like being on Secret Millionaire when you had to live undercover and how did it affect you?"

My answer is always the same.

The greatest gift you can have is when you simply give in order to help and serve others. There is no better feeling than when you know you have made a positive difference in lives of others.

FORWARD TO SMILING THROUGH RETIREMENT BY JAMES MALINCHAK

And that is **exactly** what Brian Gray and Ray Stein and their wisdom, teachings and life experiences can do for you! Brian and Ray truly care about making a positive difference in the lives of others.

Some strategies may comfort you while others may challenge your old paradigm. One thing is for certain, Brian and Ray will stamp your spirit with an abundance of knowledge and encouragement.

It is my sincere honor to introduce you to Brian and Ray and their book!

-James Malinchak
Featured on ABCs Hit TV Show, "Secret Millionaire"
Authored 20 Books, Delivered 3,000 Presentations & 1,000 Consultations
Best-Selling Author, Millionaire Success Secrets
Founder, www.MillionaireFreeBook.com

Twenty years from now you will be more disappointed by the things that you didn't do than by the ones you did do. So throw away the bowlines. Sail away from the safe harbor. Catch the trade winds in your sails. Explore, Dream. Discover.

— Mark Twain

A PERSONAL STORY IN WHAT DRIVES US

As planners, we see so many things that will change a plan. We see time and time again that people have done an excellent job saving and that they just have a tough time reaching into their savings to live life. It has actually been the hardest thing we do as planners…to get people to spend their money. We spend 30 to 40 years saving for the future, for retirement, and when we finally get there our mind still thinks our savings is for the future.

Change your thinking immediately. The future is now. If you don't spend your hard-earned savings, then you're kids and grandkids sure won't have a hard time spending it.

We all have dreams of things that we would like to do in retirement. More travel, our dream car, a dream home or buying a membership to the country club. The key is if you plan properly, you can achieve all your retirement dreams.

One question we ask everyone who comes to see us is: "Do you want the day you die to be the day your children retire?"

That's right. It is ok to spend your money as long as you have a plan to do so safely.

Ask yourself, have you ever made a financial decision that you have regretted? Of course you have. Over and over we see that there are a lot of missing critical facts, missing information, misinterpretation of advice which comes to us in lots of media forms. Newspapers, internet, magazines, television, current advisors and, ultimately, our family and friends.

Our goal in writing this book is to give you all the missing critical facts, identify the misinformation and provide you with options you may never have known existed. This way you can make more informed decisions in your financial life to help lower your stress and anxiety during your retirement years. After all, if you could know the facts before making important decisions, you'll never have to say that you wished you did something different.

You have one chance to get retirement right and having a plan that addresses these issues upfront will allow you to start living life without any regret.

Follow Mark Twain's advice to set your sails and catch the trade winds.

TABLE OF CONTENTS

Chapter 1:	Live Life in Five Year Increments	11
Chapter 2:	The Planning Process – Your Road Map to Living Life in Five Year Increments	15
Chapter 3:	Working with the Right Advisor?	19
Chapter 4:	Income Planning	21
Chapter 5:	Front Load Your Expenses	23
Chapter 6:	Social Security Income	25
Chapter 7:	Running Out of Money is Your Biggest Risk	33
Chapter 8:	Guaranteed vs. Non-Guaranteed Income	37
Chapter 9:	Market Cycles	43
Chapter 10:	Why Buy and Hold Exists	47
Chapter 11:	Tactical Strategies	49
Chapter 12:	The Importance of Minimizing Losses	51
Chapter 13:	Understanding the True Meaning of Returns "Real vs. Average"	53
Chapter 14:	Sequence of Return Risk	57
Chapter 15:	Healthcare	61
Chapter 16:	Have A Long-Term Care Plan	65
Chapter 17:	Tax-Efficiency Planning	69
Chapter 18:	Charitable and Philanthropic Planning	75
Chapter 19:	Financial Estate Planning	77
Chapter 20:	Find Your Life Print	81

CHAPTER 1
LIVE LIFE IN FIVE YEAR INCREMENTS

"I wish we spent more money in our 60s and 70s because now, our bodies don't allow us to travel the world or take the adventures we always dreamed of." Don't let these be your words in your 80s. Too many people today put off their true lifetime dreams and goals for a later date. What happens is their health finally decides for them what they can no longer do and the goals they have been planning their entire life stay on a piece of paper, never becoming reality. This leads to the disappointment Mark Twain was talking about a few pages ago.

If there is just one concept that you take away from reading this book, make it "Live Life in Five Year Increments." Do you know what you want to do in retirement? What is on your bucket list? Is your bucket list written down? Is it priced out?

Let us provide you with one of our favorite examples from a current client which we'll nickname Joan. Joan's family is everything to her, so she has found an amazing way to enjoy time with her family. Every three years, Joan rents a luxurious home in Southern California and pays for all of her children and eight grandchildren to come out for a two-week period. All expenses are paid for, so the family doesn't have to worry about a dime. Now, this does cost a good amount of money to Joan, but she tells us every time that the memories and experiences she creates, and more importantly, her children and grandchildren create and share with her about their trips to California with grandma for many years in the future are truly priceless.

World travel, golf, tennis, time with our spouse, time with your children or grandchildren, volunteer work, gardening, diving in an exotic location, exercise program, dream kitchen, dream home, quilting, knitting, woodworking, painting, reading, going to more movies, dinner with friends, and so on. Take the time now to really figure out what makes life worth living for you and your spouse. What memories do you want to create and fulfil in your life? What life print do you want to leave for your family and society?

Now, how does this fit into living life in five-year increments? When many people think of retirement, they think they have 20 to 30 years where they evenly spend money. But how does life really work? At some point, health starts to creep in… slowly or sometimes quickly.

Life has a way of throwing us a curve ball when we least expect it. One day we are healthy and the next day we are not. Our spouse can have their health deteriorate. We lose our spouse unexpectedly. The market corrects and takes away some of your hard-earned savings.

Start today by planning life in five-year increments. We call these the Go-Go, Slow-Go and No-Go years. Front-load your spending into the first five years of retirement, your Go-Go Years, to do the big bucket list items that require your best health. We always joke in our classes that Europe and South America were not made for wheelchairs and walkers, so you should visit them while you're still mobile.

After your Go-Go Years you will enter your Slow-Go Years. This typically will be somewhere in your mid 70s as we will naturally start to slow down. You will still have some big bucket list items to complete and you will start tackling more of your medium-size bucket list items, such as more local travel in the United States. Continue to plan this way as eventually, health will catch up to you in the No-Go Years.

When you get into your 80s, most of life revolves around the limitations of your health and doctor appointments. These will be your No-Go Years. Now, don't get us wrong, these can still be amazing years, however, most people in their 80s are not able to travel the world and hike mountains anymore. The finances at this point should be setup and discussions are usually around how to best leave a legacy to the future generation while paying the least amount of taxes.

Our goal in this book is to make sure you have achieved your lifetime goals throughout retirement without major stress, anxiety, or regret and planning to live your life in five-year increments is the first step.

Have you ever made a financial decision that you have regretted? Absolutely, we all have. We will help you gather all the missing information, the missing critical facts and clear up the myths in retirement planning so you can make more informed decisions and not have future regrets.

Throughout the rest of this book, we will walk you through how to think about your investment portfolio, your income plan, healthcare, taxes and estate plan in a five-year increment philosophy. We want you to have the best chances of checking off every retirement, no, life goal, you have without the worry of running out of money.

Planning for the items in the rest of this book will help you smile through retirement.

CHAPTER 2
THE PLANNING PROCESS YOUR ROAD MAP TO LIVING LIFE IN FIVE YEAR INCREMENTS

We have a saying in our firm. "Have a plan. Have a plan. Have a plan." Sounds silly, right? It is as important as in real estate. "Location. Location. Location."

If you were to fly to Florida for a warm winter vacation would you just go to the airport and buy a ticket? To do it right you would research flight times and costs. Then you would figure out hotel accommodations and best yet, what type of car to rent. Then you would figure out what beach or attractions to visit and what restaurants you want to eat at. And most importantly, figure out what you are willing to spend.

Not many advisors specialize in retirement planning. It can be hard to find one that will look at your entire picture and walk you through the process of having a plan so you can live your life in those five-year increments.

Most of the online financial planning software available today doesn't consider living life in five-year increments. Most will ask for monthly or annual expenses, then grow that amount with an inflation rate keeping your spending constant. The problem with online calculators is that people don't just spend a constant amount each month. And we haven't found one that will allow you to spend more in your Go-Go Years to accomplish your bucket list. Nor one that will lower those expenses during the Slow-Go or No-Go Years. It is important to front load your spending so you can maintain your lifestyle. However, it is important to not spend too much early on.

Therefore, we created the five-step retirement process which will pick up most of the risk you will face in retirement. All five steps are important, however, the first two are critical in getting right to help ensure a successful retirement. These are the income planning step and the protecting savings step. We will dedicate a couple chapters to each to go into more specifics.

1st Step - Protecting your nest egg is important because the rest of the steps depend on if you spend or lose your assets. This includes protecting your assets from losses due to major market corrections, lawsuits, liens and judgments.

2nd Step - Income Planning is an important process as you can only spend income in retirement, not savings. If you have secured income you can absorb other risk in retirement.

3rd Step - Medical costs and Medicare decisions need to be made, as well as looking at your family's solution to addressing the possible need for long-term care. We all know it only takes one major medical issue to arise to deplete our assets if the proper insurance isn't in place.

4th Step - All decisions here impact the taxes you will pay throughout retirement. Would it surprise you to know that most taxes are voluntary? Having a good tax plan is essential to keeping the most of your retirement savings.

5th Step - Having a financial estate plan will tie everything up in a bow to make sure what money and assets are left are used in the way you truly intended. Most estate plans make sure the right people get it. A good plan will also address that the right amount goes to the right people at the right time. This also allows you to create your life print.

There is always a cost to do something and a cost to do nothing. It is our goal to help provide you with a framework to make more informed decisions moving forward by shedding the light on all the pros and cons of your financial decisions.

CHAPTER 3
WORKING WITH THE RIGHT ADVISOR?

Retirement is like a baseball game. Back in the 70s and 80s, a starting pitcher would pitch all nine innings 19 to 20 times each season. Today a starting pitcher will last between five or six innings before the relief pitchers come in. Most teams end the last inning with a closer. If you look at your life the years you saved for retirement you may have been working with a starting pitcher. Most advisors do an excellent job getting you ready to start your retirement, however, they are limited in their ability to get you to the end of the game. Many use the same rules they used to help you save, but those rules are different in the later stage of life. Here are some things to consider in finding that late inning or closing pitcher. We call this outgrowing your current advisors' capabilities.

Fiduciary vs. Suitability

You should be aware that there are two standards for advisors when selecting an advisor that will help you save and plan for retirement. Why is this important? This is your retirement and any advisor that doesn't plan for all possibilities in retirement may not be the right person to help you plan your retirement.

First, let's provide the definition of each.

Fiduciary: A legal obligation of one party to act in the best interest of another. This means the advisor must hold the client's interest above its own in all matters at all times.

Suitability: Brokers are obligated to make sure the securities they recommend are suitable for clients based upon factors such as the client's risk tolerance, age, and investment goals.

Tony Robbins, the motivational speaker and author, spent a few chapters in his book "Money, Master the Game" outlining why you should work with a fiduciary. Most former SEC (Securities and Exchange Commission) chairpersons have said to make sure you work with a fiduciary.

Arthur Levitt, a former SEC Chairman, wrote in great detail in his book titled "Take On The Street: How to Fight for your Financial Future" about the problems of the suitability standard and the brokerage business model.

The main reason is that the fiduciary must always look out for your best interest. A person who is employed by a Wall Street brokerage firm has to put clients into products that are best for the firm and not always the best for a client.

As of the writing of this book, the Department of Labor is proposing to make anyone who handles a retirement account like a 401(k) plan and IRA to act as a fiduciary and use a Best Interest Contract as a possible solution.

The SEC is also looking into requiring that all advisors be fiduciaries. We do feel that every financial advisor should act and be held to a higher level and would hope the industry moves in that direction as soon as possible.

The main issue is when a broker works with your retirement accounts, they must work with your best interest in mind. What about your other non-retirement accounts? Most suitable advisors only focus on investments and leave it up to you to figure out Social Security choices, Medicare choices and tax planning. No wonder so many people are afraid of running out of money in retirement!

We point this out because Boston based Aite Group studies the financial industry and recognizes that about 10% of all advisors are full fiduciary advisors and the other 90% fall under the suitability standard.

Ask yourself: Do you want to work with a fiduciary for all your retirement needs? If so, you need to consider a change of advisors. Look for the late inning relief pitcher or closer that strives to get you a win in your retirement.

CHAPTER 4
INCOME PLANNING

Remember the Bugs Bunny Cartoons? In five of the cartoons, Wile E. Coyote tried to outsmart good old Bugs. One episode features Wile in a TNT shack filling up carrots with explosive powder. While this is happening, Bugs Bunny takes a tractor and pulls the TNT shack onto the railroad tracks. Next you see a train coming around the mountain. When Wile sees the train coming all he can do is pull down the shade in the window and hope the train doesn't hit him. Well you know what happened next. The shack blew up and the wise coyote wound up hanging from a tree branch on the side of a cliff.

Don't be a coyote. Don't let hope be your retirement plan.

Are you setup with a retirement pension plan at work that covers 80% to 100% of your earnings? If you are like most Americans, your answer is a resounding NO. Unfortunately pension plans began disappearing in the mid-80s due to the rise of the ultimate retirement trap, the 401(k) plan. Instead of your employer being responsible for your retirement income, they chose to pass that responsibility on to you through a defined contribution plan aka 401(k). Declining pension plans and the growing financial issues Social Security is facing (which we will discuss later) are two of the main reasons those facing retirement today will not have enough income to maintain their standard of living.

You can have a large "nest egg" saved in retirement accounts such as 401(k)s and IRAs, however they can provide you no benefit until you turn them into income. The largest issue with taking money from your retirement plans (other than Roth IRAs) is the taxes you owe on each dollar coming out. We will dive into the complexities of taxes and how to plan for them in a later chapter. Other than taxes, several other issues come into play such as how much to withdraw, what will your investment returns be, what will you do if you take large investment losses, should you turn some of your funds into guaranteed income not susceptible to stock market losses?

The importance of having a good income plan will keep you from hanging on the side of the cliff outsmarted by life. For most of us, our income in retirement consists of Social Security, maybe a pension or two and living off our savings. If this covers our expenses, then all is good in retirement in covering our expenses.

What we see is that people who have their income sources guaranteed live a happier, lower stress retirement. Those that rely on the fluctuation of the market typically have more stress and tend to not live their life the way they would like to. Remember, in order to live life in five-year increments you need a good income plan to help you get there. Ask yourself, do you want a sure thing or a maybe?

A good income plan will include your day-to-day expenses, (food, clothing, shelter), your fun (entertainment, travel etc.), tithing (charities and/or church) medical costs (premiums and co-pays) and taxes. If you have all your expenses covered on a guaranteed basis, then you will lower your stress and live your life and complete your bucket list.

Parts of a good income plan will take into consideration things that could change during your retirement. What will your income look like if you lose your life partner? What will happen if taxes go up? What will happen if you need to care for a parent or child or grandchild? What is your plan if Social Security does drop your Social Security income in 2034 by 21%? What about rising Medicare premiums?

Finding a good retirement planner will help create a plan that you can get most of your income set up on a guaranteed basis to help lower any stress level.

CHAPTER 5
FRONT LOAD YOUR EXPENSES

Opportunities are like sunrises. If you wait too long, you miss them. – William Arthur Ward

"Why didn't we enjoy it while we had it?" Mrs. Magpie asked her husband with sorrow. You see, the Magpies spent their entire careers saving and putting away for a rainy day, proudly working well past age 65 and into their 70s. Mrs. Magpie had always wanted to see Europe, to tour the vineyards of France, the castles of Germany and float down the canals of Venice, Italy. Mr. Magpie had always dreamed of buying that classic Camaro and cruising the coast of California.

The Magpies would save, save and save, looking at their retirement accounts with pride as they grew and grew. One day, however Mr. Magpie suddenly had a stroke. He had to stop working and lost his ability to walk. Their dreams suddenly vanished. Mrs. Magpie would never travel without her husband who could now only get around in a wheelchair and he certainly could never drive again. Although they had saved millions, it was of little value to them now as their dreams had been stolen by time and health.

This story is today's example of a couple reaching retirement who make the same mistake portrayed in Aesop's fable about the Miser who put his life savings into a nugget of gold which he then buried, never used and had stolen from him. We see too many retirees today who have this mindset. They fear spending money and living life in the now. Health will eventually catch up to all of us, so we must make the most of today, our healthiest years.

Aesop's other fable, "The Goose That Laid the Golden Eggs," reminds us that you cannot also spend too much too early, or you risk killing your retirement goose that needs to last the rest of your life. A well thought out plan must be in place to provide for the Go-Go Years through the No-Go Years.

There is a prime period between the ages of 59½ and 70½ where you should consider spending more money. These years are usually the healthiest years of retirement and it can help you spend down some retirement assets early before the Internal Revenue Service (IRS) forces you to take money out through Required Minimum Distributions, which we talk about in the chapter on taxes.

What if you were able to retire earlier than you thought? How about starting Social Security at 62, setting up other guaranteed income to begin at 62 as well and now all of your expenses are covered. You then divide a portion of your retirement savings into five year increments. For the first five years, you pull out of your IRA accounts at a high rate to enjoy life. The next five years money grows over that time so that, at age 67, you can add more guaranteed income. Finally, the last part of your income plan is money that has grown in guaranteed or non-guaranteed investments over 10 or 15 years to cover the No-Go and Slow-Go Years. You also have the choice to make your future income taxable or tax-free which we dive into during our tax chapter. Now this is a much better plan than never spending money like the Magpie couple did at the beginning of this chapter.

Remember to front load your spending during your Go-Go Years but also have a plan that shows the effect on the latter years in life so you don't risk over doing it.

CHAPTER 6
SOCIAL SECURITY INCOME

When should I claim Social Security benefits? Is Social Security even going to be able to pay me? These are two of the most common questions people ask about Social Security and they are valid questions as every Social Security statement says that the system will become insolvent by the year 2034!

A couple that we met had a heartbreaking story to tell about their experience with taking Social Security. When they were both age 62, they heard from work colleagues and a CPA friend that they should take Social Security benefits right away because it "wouldn't be there for them" in the future. So this couple added up their expenses and realized that the lower benefit amounts they could take at age 62 would cover all their expenses, plus they had a few years' worth of savings in their 401(k) plans at work. They both decided to retire from work early and take Social Security.

Now it is eight years later and this couple is coming to us for help. They had spent the last eight years spending not only Social Security benefits (since those just covered basic expenses), but they also had to tap into their savings and were almost out. Instead of thriving and enjoying their retirement years, they were just barely getting by and they are now trying to find new jobs… in their 70s! This story and many others like it are why we are passionate about making sure you have a true income plan in retirement and that starts with evaluating your cash flow needs now as well as in the future. Now, is Social Security even going to be around for you? You've heard it's going broke, right?

Social Security is in Trouble

The Social Security Trustees are trying to get the word out on page 2 of your Social Security statement, that if nothing is done to fix the system, they are going to have to cut benefits to everyone by at least 21% in 2034. We don't know about you, but we wouldn't accept such a large pay cut at work and those in retirement shouldn't accept this either. The following chart from the 2016 OASDI Trustees report shows the trust fund is estimated to be depleted in 2034 and payable benefits will have to fall to 79%, meaning everyone takes a 21% pay cut to keep the system going... yikes!

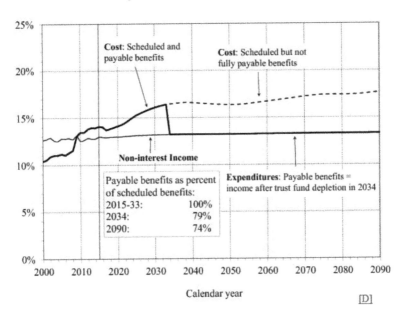

Source: 2016 OASDI Trustees Report
https://www.ssa.gov/oact/tr/2016/II_D_project.html#105057

There are many "fixes" that are being studied today which could help make Social Security more solvent. They include increasing or removing the cap on earnings paid into Social Security, delaying the age to which future beneficiaries can start Social Security payments and decreasing benefits to future generations. This last option is the most likely as workers in their 30s and 40s don't even expect to get much from Social Security when they retire. For politicians, this is probably the easiest route and it avoids a fight with those in retirement who often vote the most.

For this reason, most agree that if you are around age 50 or older, you can count on your current estimated Social Security benefits being there for you.

Now let's get to looking at how we can answer the important question of when should you start your Social Security benefits and if you should or shouldn't focus on maximizing them.

Social Security benefits are vitally important to most retirement plans because the benefits offer a lifetime income with an inflation increase (although not guaranteed every year) called a Cost of Living Adjustment or COLA. This means that if you live to age 100, Social Security will continue to pay you and you will likely receive larger checks every year, especially if we have inflation. It is hard to find these types of guarantees elsewhere.

Betting Your Life

Taking Social Security too early risks you not having enough cash flow in later years, but a larger risk may be waiting too long. What are the chances of your health declining before age 70? Pretty high and Social Security knows this; a larger portion of retirees won't make it to age 70 and Social Security will win the bet. Did you know that adults aged 50-74 account for over half (53%) of all new cancer cases?[1]

Remember the five-year increments we recommend you living your life by? If you are putting off that vacation of a lifetime, taking the grandkids to Disney, starting that hobby, or whatever makes your life worth living until 66 or 70, remember that **you are risking the healthiest years of your life**. Therefore, Social Security timing is so important and it depends on factors that impact the rest of your life. Among these factors are life expectancy, current health, your spouse's or partner's current health and life expectancy, your family's health history, current and future cash flows, taxes, estate/family planning and a host of other important items we talk about in this book.

As a general guideline, remember that anytime you take benefits before your Normal Retirement Age, or NRA (shown as age 66 to 67 on your Social Security statement), you are taking a haircut of as much as 30% of your income for the rest of your life!

What does Social Security want you to do? Mathematically, the answer is....DIE. When we teach our Social Security classes, most of our attendees laugh when we say this; however, it's true. If you die early, all the money you paid in to the system can now go to someone else and help perpetuate the system. So, Social Security has devised a way to keep betting on your life with you. If you wait past your NRA, Social Security will offer you a guaranteed 8% annual credit plus COLA until you reach age 70. That is a minimum of 32% growth of your income, but there is a big IF....You stay alive. Not only alive, but you want to be in good enough health to spend that money as well. It makes no sense to have extra cash flow if your health is not good enough to actually enjoy it.

In addition, if you are married, divorced, are a widow/widower, disabled or a young dependent, there are many different timing strategies you want to consider. For example, did you know that if one or both spouses are over the age of 62, that one spouse can take their benefit at 66, let the other spouse take their spousal benefit at 66 and then switch to their own benefit at 70, collecting all the years of 8% delayed credits? Did you know widows/widowers have a similar option starting as early as age 60 even if they were divorced from a marriage of over 10 years?

Survivor Benefits

The Survivor benefit is also an area that we want to make sure people understand as most don't realize what a large effect on income the death of a spouse can have on Social Security benefits alone. The general rule after you have both taken Social Security is that when either spouse passes away, the lower of the two benefits is gone. Social Security will allow the higher of the two benefits to remain, however there is still usually a major loss of income to the household. Let's look at a simple example below:

SPOUSE 1
Annual SS Benefit
$24,000

SPOUSE 2
Annual SS Benefit
$20,000

COMBINED
Annual SS Benefit
$44,000

Loss of Benefit after either spouse passes away:
($20,000)

% Loss of Social Security Income to household:
45.45% ⬇

Not only is the surviving spouse recovering from losing his/her life partner, but they have to deal with a pay cut! If the survivor wasn't the spouse handling the finances, are they going to know where/how to pull investments or how to change investments to come up with their loss of income? Are expenses really going to drop by a large amount for the survivor especially if that spouse is not spending money to not be alone – dining out with friends/family, travelling or any other increased expenses to help with the emotional recovery from their loss? In our experience with clients who have lost a spouse, spending actually tends to increase over time and we want to make sure that the surviving spouse is able to spend more instead of worrying about having to spend less and running out of retirement funds.

Remember the couple that both took their Social Security at 62 and they are now just surviving on their benefits. The survivor is going to be in a world of hurt when the first one dies. Losing income that will take them below their expenses with no retirement savings left. The survivor's options become limited. The survivor can sell the home, do a reverse mortgage, take on roommates, move in with the kids or vice versa. We suggest having a plan that addresses the loss of Social Security income.

Taxes

Did you know that prior to 1983 Social Security income was 100% TAX FREE?[2] Unfortunately today, there is a tax schedule and most people have a majority of their Social Security income added to their AGI (adjusted gross income) and taxable every year. In the current Social Security tax schedule if your income goes above a certain threshold ($34,000 as an individual and $44,000 joint) 85% of your Social Security income is taxable. Social Security has a nasty trick up its sleeve as well, the Social Security Administration uses modified AGI which makes it easier to get above these thresholds. What is modified AGI? "Modified AGI is AGI plus nontaxable interest income plus income from foreign sources plus one-half of Social Security benefits."[3] his means that if your advisor has you in municipal bonds for tax-free interest income or some foreign income, this is added to your modified AGI.

Is it possible to make your Social Security income tax free? Yes! However, it takes a great deal of planning because you need to find other sources of income which we will discuss in this book to get your modified AGI below the Social Security taxable thresholds. It is possible, but careful planning usually over multiple years is required. Make sure you have an advisor and CPA team who are familiar with how these rules work.

Find the Right Advisor Team

This chapter is not designed to go into the nuances of each of the thousands of Social Security rules that may or may not apply to you; however, we recommend that you meet with a fiduciary advisor who can assist you in discovering all the benefits that may apply to you and your family. The Social Security office is not allowed to do this type of planning for you as they are instructed not to help determine strategies to get more from Social Security. It's like asking the IRS for tax advice…probably not going to happen.

CHAPTER 7
RUNNING OUT OF MONEY IS YOUR BIGGEST RISK

Why do people run out of money in retirement? What happens when they fall short on their plans? What can people do today to avoid or plan for these risks? These are important questions that you should address when looking at your retirement plan. Knowing the risks and having a plan for each can help you avoid running out of money in retirement, having to cancel your travel and fun plans, or worse yet, having to go back to work!

Longevity Risk – You May Have Many Years to Live

What is your largest risk to running out of money in retirement? Many would say healthcare costs or Social Security not being able to pay benefits. However the largest risk in retirement is longevity. Longevity is the multiplier of risks as the longer you live, the longer you must face and plan for the possibility of the other risks in retirement happening to you. Retirees are living much longer today than they did in the past. In 1935 when Social Security was developed, the average life expectancy was 61 years old and most retirees only planned on a 10- to 15-year retirement.[4]

Today, the Centers for Disease Control and Prevention estimates U.S. life expectancy at 78.8 years.[5] This is just an average. A good majority of retirees will live beyond this amount, so planning on a 20- to 30-year retirement is a good idea. You probably don't want to live to age 100, but making sure that you can make it there and beyond financially is an important step in the planning process. You want to make sure that you don't have to move in with the kids or grandkids.

After longevity risk, the Society of Actuaries identified 15 areas of post-retirement risk that many retirees face with an emphasis on inflation, interest rates, stock market, public policy (e.g. taxes) and unexpected healthcare needs & costs.[6] Another risk of note for couples is the emotional and financial hardship that can follow the loss of a spouse.

Inflation Risk – Costs Will Rise in the Future

In the absence of the gold standard, there is no way to protect savings from confiscation through inflation. There is no safe store of value.
–Alan Greenspan, Former Federal Reserve Chairman

Inflation risk is the risk of today's prices increasing over time and has the potential to wreak havoc to anyone on a fixed income. Looking at it from a purely mathematical perspective, if inflation averages 4%, purchasing power can be cut in half in only 18 years. If inflation levels reach the levels they did in the 70s and early 80s of 10% to 14%, then retirees need to have a way to increase their cashflow accordingly or risk a significant decrease in their standard of living.[7] You may want to consider having some inflation protection in your portfolio such as Treasury Inflation Protected Securities and having a plan to maximize Social Security benefits as they have built in Cost of Living Adjustments which we discussed in the Social Security chapter. Equities have traditionally outpaced inflation, so keeping some higher risk assets in retirement may be a good idea. You just need to have a protection plan in place which we will also discuss in a later chapter.

Interest Rate Risk – Why Own CDs Today?

Interest rates have continued to fall around the world and with today's low rates, retirees face a unique challenge – where can they put their money to earn a return and provide safety from stock market corrections? In the past CDs, or bank Certificates of Deposit provided an appropriate solution as their returns beat long term inflation and provided safety. However, with the fall of interest rates, many CDs are paying less than 1% per year. With the fact that you are forced to tie your money up for at least three to five years in CDs, many retirees are looking elsewhere.

Retirees have also depended on corporate bond returns in the past to provide a solid source of level income. Bond rates have also continued to fall and today, 80% of the world's bonds are paying less than 4% interest per year. This is just a small amount above inflation and when you consider taxes you must pay on the earnings, you may not be able to beat inflation over time. When interest rates rise the bonds will be subject to declining in value

Stock Market Risk – Remember 2008 and 2000-2002?

Stocks can only move in three directions: up, down and sideways. Most people are only set up to do well when stocks go up, so when the stock market has a normal correction of over 30% every five to seven years, their retirement income can be devastated. This is such an important risk, that we have created an entire chapter on market risk and how to help protect your life savings later in the book. We don't like when they say a stock market needs a correction. After all, why correct something that is working?

Public Policy Risk – Are Taxes Going Up or Down?

With over $20 trillion in debt, the United States (and the rest of the world) needs to figure out how to repay its outstanding loans. One way for the government to do this is to increase taxes over time through various means. This is a huge risk for retirees as Social Security can be taxable, Medicare has extra premiums if you have more income and all retirement accounts (except Roth IRAs and Roth 401(k)s are taxable as you pull the funds out. And by the way, if you don't pull the funds out, the IRS forces you to at the age of 70½ in the form of Required Minimum Distributions, or RMDs. Tax planning should be done every year along with forward tax planning to address issues of moving into higher tax brackets later in life. Again, this is an important topic which we will discuss in greater detail.

Unexpected Healthcare Needs & Cost Risk – Are You Covered for Major Medical Expenses?

Healthcare costs are one of the largest sources of worry for those in and nearing retirement in the United States. As our health naturally declines, expenses tend to increase. Making sure that you have the proper insurance is vital to covering the potential of large health expenses. Prior to age 65, your health insurance may be covered in several ways such as by your employer plan, religious plan, COBRA or, under current law, the Affordable Care Act (Obamacare). Once you reach 65, you can sign up for Medicare to cover normal health costs, but what is not covered is long-term recovery expenses and nursing expenses. A long-term care insurance plan can help to cover these costs which can be large. A nursing home costs between $8,000 to $10,000 each month for full-time care. In its most recent survey of those in retirement, the Society of Actuaries identified long-term care expenses as the largest source of surprise expenses in retirement.

Loss of a Spouse – Are You Both Going to be Financially OK?

The loss of a spouse can be one of the hardest emotional events to go through, especially if it is early and unexpected. In addition to losing your best friend, most surviving spouses lose a large portion of their guaranteed lifetime income. For example, the general rule with Social Security benefits is the lower of the two benefits goes away. If you both have a similar benefit, say $2,000/month, that is a 50% reduction in Social Security income. Pensions can have similar rules where the survivor is left with a pay cut or no income at all.

Do you or your spouse mainly handle the finances and investments? If your spouse is left to deal with all the choices of how to handle the money, pay bills, and chose new investments, would they be comfortable with that? Having a plan to take care of the surviving spouse and make sure they know where to go for help will be a tremendous benefit to the survivor in the future.

CHAPTER 8
GUARANTEED VS. NON-GUARANTEED INCOME

Ask yourself this. When you retire do you want your income to be a "sure thing" or a "maybe"?

What if there was a way to turn part of your savings into a sure thing? A sure thing is guaranteed income which would pay you for the rest of your life no matter if the market went down? All income can be broken down into two basic forms, guaranteed (Sure Thing) and not guaranteed (Maybe). Sounds pretty simple, right? Although it sounds simple, too many people today have their income setup almost entirely with non-guaranteed sources.

Have you talked to someone who has all their expenses plus some covered with a pension and Social Security? They are generally very happy in retirement because they know they can have fun and enjoy life without having to worry about what news event or politician could crash the market this week. Guaranteed income should be setup at a minimum to cover your basic essential expenses such as mortgage/rent, food, clothing and taxes. To go a step further, you can setup additional guaranteed income sources to cover vacations, dining, visiting family or any other important activities you don't want tied to the risks of the stock or bond markets. Once you figure out your essential expenses, including travel or other important items, you want to make sure your guaranteed income covers all these items or gets as close as possible. The rest of the money can then be setup to take more risk in the markets since you have all the necessities covered through guaranteed income.

We have a simple philosophy we follow in income planning. Buy or secure your income and invest the difference. If you have your income guaranteed then you can take on some investment risk without worry about your income. Does this make sense?

An easy way to figure out which type of income you have is to ask this question: Can the income value change due to poor performance of the underlying vehicle? (Such as dividends on stocks, interest on bonds or capital appreciation). If the answer is yes and there is a possibility the income stream can change in value, then that income steam is not guaranteed. Most advisors today who focus solely on investments use a defunct and faulty rule of thumb called the 4% rule which we go into more detail about later in the book. The reason these advisors use this rule is because they are focused on keeping you in a 100% market risk portfolio and they cannot guarantee any sort of return or, therefore, income in retirement. They are "hoping" the market will get you enough gains to fuel your income needs and we do not like to have "hope" as the foundation of a retirement plan.

Guaranteed income can come in many forms such as Social Security, pensions, structured settlements, lottery payouts and annuities from life insurance companies. We are going to cover several types of annuities. Whether you have heard good things or bad things about annuities, a select few can offer some good opportunities like the ability to offer secure income in the right situation for those in retirement.

There are two general types of annuities: immediate or deferred. Their name describes what they do as an immediate annuity starts lifetime guaranteed income payments to you immediately (usually within 30 days) after giving the insurance company a lump sum of money. This is a good option if you need income sooner and have done a decent job saving money to this point. If you have some time to wait, you can let the insurance company defer the annuity funds with the chance of growth.

With a deferred annuity, you give the insurance company a lump sum of money now with the intention of taking income sometime in the future (usually 5 to 10 years from now). Why would you do this? There is the chance for growth of these funds and therefore growth in your future guaranteed income stream. Similar to Social Security benefits, the longer you wait, generally the more money you get in income. But how do those funds grow? There are several types of deferred annuities available including fixed rate, indexed, and variable annuities.

A fixed, fixed rate, or multiyear guaranteed annuity offers you a guaranteed rate of interest over a specified number of years. A large benefit to this annuity is the fact that there is zero stock or bond market risk. Compared to a bank CD, they have many similarities, however some benefits of the fixed annuity include the ability for the gains to compound every year (CDs make you take out interest each year), for tax-deferred growth. Usually there are no fees unless you take out more than 10% of the value of the annuity including the growth in a year. These annuities can be a great alternative to those who love CDs as life insurance companies can generally offer higher interest rates than those found in CDs. In a low interest-rate environment such as we have at the time of this writing, fixed annuities may not offer the returns many investors are looking for.

The fixed indexed annuity was designed back in 1995 to provide retirees with a vehicle that has no market risk with the possibility of more gains over time. This type of annuity lets you decide to have your gains (also known as crediting) be linked to an index such as the S&P 500 or a fixed rate which you have the option to switch between annually in most cases.

The life insurance company is able to offer you no market risk with more upside potential through indexing. Although you don't get all the upside potential of the market, you can still get most of it while at the same time avoiding the chance of going backwards. For example, if the index you are using is the S&P 500 and it goes down 20% over the annual term of your annuity, you would get credited zero, but more importantly, you would not have gone backwards at all! This is a powerful concept, especially when you include only the upside gain potential over the term of your annuity.

The following chart shows an example of a fixed indexed annuity that started in 1998 with the red line representing the S&P 500 index and the green line representing the cash value of the annuity. Notice how in 2000 through 2002, the green line stayed flat. The same is true from 2007 to 2009. How much further ahead would you be today if you hadn't gone backwards during the last two down markets?

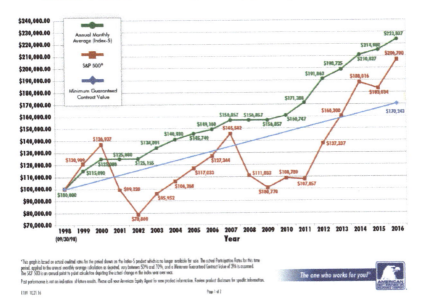

While the fixed indexed annuity offers many great benefits, you still want to think about it as offering moderate returns over time in your planning. You do have the chance of some great up years, but since there are no guarantees on the upside, just guarantees against market loss, you want to keep your estimates conservative. Over time, you have the chance for good growth that can then be turned into a larger income stream than if you had started earlier.

The final type of annuity is called a variable annuity and just as the name applies, your funds can vary to the upside, but more importantly they can lose value due to market losses. Funds within a variable annuity are invested in sub accounts which are then typically invested into mutual funds. When the underlying investments lose money, so does your annuity which is the main reason we are not fans of variable annuities in retirement planning. We would like to base your plan on more guarantees than a foundation that varies. Another issue we have with variable annuities is they generally have a higher fee structure for their clients. The advisor has to get paid, the mutual fund managers have to get paid and the insurance company has to get paid. With all the levels of management, the average variable annuity fees are estimated to be as high as 3%-4% per year or more![8] The combination of market risks and high fees often make variable annuities the wrong choice for most people in retirement.

Some items you want to consider before purchasing any annuity are the term of the annuity, the surrender charges during that term, the liquidity of the annuity (most annuities let you take out 7%-10% of the money you put in plus any gains every year), and the financial strength of the insurance company. Also be sure you understand the formulas for calculating your annual gains as some insurance companies offer many options with different variations. A good rule to live by is keep it simple. If you don't understand it fully, it may not be the best option for you. We generally like simple, easy to understand annuities that you can calculate yourself if you want to. In addition, make sure you are working with a fiduciary advisor that is also independent. Ask them to show you how they shopped around for the best annuity and compare their top choices with you. Also, you will want to find annuities offered by investment grade life Insurance companies. This will minimize the risk of the company going out of business.[9]

When you are looking at income planning, you want to take stock of your income year by year after retirement. For example, if you retire at age 62, how long can you wait before starting Social Security? If you plan on maximizing your Social Security benefits at age 70, you may want to look at starting annuity income before then to cover cash flow needs until 70. Or vice versa, you can start Social Security at age 62 while letting a deferred annuity grow until 66 or 70 which may offer a larger income stream later.

Also keep in mind that if you are a couple, should an accident or illness cause one of you to pass away early, the smaller of the two Social Security benefits goes away. A deferred annuity can be a good option to back fill the loss of Social Security income should one person pass away early. The income stream can be turned on to cover the loss, or left to grow until needed at the choice of the surviving spouse.

Many tools are available to help cover your guaranteed income so you want to identify the amounts and the years where you may need more or less income. Planning can be done to cover these years and also allow for more income in later years as well.

CHAPTER 9
MARKET CYCLES
What goes up must go down – Isaac Newton

Do you think a 2008 event can happen again? When we ask this question in our retirement courses we see a resounding response of hands that do think this will happen again. The problem is major market corrections happen more times than we usually remember. Again, why do we need a correction when the market is working?

It is called market cycles. Have you ever been taught what a market cycle is? Or asked what the heck is a market cycle?

A market cycle includes both a bull and a bear market. A client simplified this for us once. "In simple terms, a bull cycle is when I make money and a bear cycle is when I lose money." A typical full market cycle will average 5-7 years.

As of the writing of this book the stock market has had 22 bear market cycles since 1900. They have happened on average every 5-7 years with an average loss of 37.5%. Think about this. Once you retire, you could see losses in your investments four or five more times before you die. If you don't have a plan to address this, it can be detrimental to your retirement plan.

Here is a chart of the Dow Jones Industrial Average showing the start of all 22 bear markets since 1900. Bear markets are considered when any market corrects by around 20% or more.

Historical Start of Bear Market Corrections.
June 1901 to October 2007

If you notice the January 2000 start date, there was only a 38% loss in the Dow. Where were most of you invested back in 1999 leading up to that correction? For most of us, we were invested more in technology stocks and more exposed to the Nasdaq index which lost 76% during that time and the S&P 500 which lost over 51%.

The last two major corrections for most of us were around 50%.

We point this out because the average recovery time to get to even is about six years.

In the book "This Time is Different: Eight Centuries of Financial Folly" two leading economists, Carmen M. Reinhart and Kenneth S. Rogoff, studied all fiscal, financial and monetary crises for the last 800 years. It's hard to believe that there have been many more than the tech crash, financial crisis of 2008 and the Great Depression. In the book they detailed each crisis and market cycle and the time it took to recover and get back to even. Each time it was about six years.

The chart on the following page shows they happen more often than our brains are wired to remember.

CYCLICAL BEAR MARKET COLLAPSES

START DATE		TOTAL LOSS
1	JUNE 1901	-46%
2	JANUARY 1906	-48%
3	NOVEMBER 1909	-27%
4	OCTOBER 1912	-44%
5	NOVEMBER 1916	-40%
6	NOVEMBER 1919	-47%
7	SEPTEMBER 1929	-89%
8	MARCH 1937	-49%
9	NOVEMBER 1938	-41%
10	MAY 1946	-24%
11	JULY 1957	-19%
12	DECEMBER 1961	-27%
13	JANUARY 1966	-25%
14	DECEMBER 1968	-36%
15	JANUARY 1973	-45%
16	SEPTEMBER 1976	-27%
17	APRIL 1981	-24%
18	AUGUST 1987	-36%
19	JULY 1990	-21%
20	JULY 1998	-19%
21	JANUARY 2000	-38%
22	OCTOBER 2007	-52%

AVERAGE LOSS OF -37.5%

Source: Dow Jones

CHAPTER 10
WHY BUY AND HOLD EXISTS

Buy and hold investing also known as passive management of investments gained popularity in 1973 with the book written by Princeton economist Burton G. Malkiel called "A Random Walk Down Wall Street."

In basic terms it is an investment style in which a person will buy an asset and hold on to it for the long run. Hold on to it through good and bad market cycles. Hold onto it through the gains and losses.

Prior to 1975 less than 15% of Americans had money in the stock markets. Now, just under 80% have money invested in the market with most holdings with mutual funds in their IRAs and 401(k) accounts. Wall Street took this book and in our opinion convinced the new inexperienced investors that "Buy and Hold" is the only way to invest your money in the market. When mutual funds gained popularity in 1975, the firms had to find a way to keep you invested in their funds when the market went down.

When the markets fall what are the famous sayings our advisors, television and radio hosts and articles tell us? They have been telling us this for years.

Stay the course, the markets always come back.

When they come back, they come back higher.

It's only a paper loss until you sell it.

If you sell now you will miss the recovery.

For the most part Wall Street's advice has been correct here. But does this mean it will always be this way. Here are a few facts that are important to know for retirement planning and living your life in five-year increments. The above statements can and possibly will impact your decisions during retirement.

Buy and hold does work until it doesn't. If you were to have retired in 2000 when the stock markets took their fall it would have taken essentially 13 years to get back to even. There was a small gain in 2006. See chart.

Also from 1966 to 1982 the S&P 500 took 17 years to get back to even. The cumulative return over those 17 years was a whopping 1%. Now that's not an annual return it is the total return. Many people were not around in 1929 but it took until 1954 to get back to even. That was 25 years.

Ask yourself, if you lose 30% of your retirement dollars with market corrections will you take that large vacation? Remodel your home? Visit your family?

Keep in mind that in retirement, you have fewer years to make up for the losses to maintain the five-year increment lifestyle.

Also, those invested in Japan's Nikkei 225 index still haven't come back to even since the index's high in December 1989. As of March 1, 2016 the index was still down 56%. That was 26 years later.

In the U.S., the Nasdaq 100 hit a high in March 2000 and got back to even in February 2015. In 15 years it got back to even.

During the financial crisis, a 60% stock and 40% bond portfolio went backwards by roughly 35%. Diversification does not prevent losses during systematic losses like those experienced in the 2000-2002 and 2007-2009 periods.

Just because the Dow Jones and S&P 500 got back to even on average every six years does that mean it will always happen that way? Do you want to risk your retirement income if you need to rely on market returns for income? Remember, buy or secure income and invest the difference.

What is your plan to minimize your participation in the next market fall?

CHAPTER 11
TACTICAL STRATEGIES

Remember the last chapter on buy and hold? We'll you don't need to play that game any longer. There are tactical strategies that over time have performed well through full market cycles. The goal with investing is to minimize your exposure to market corrections, focusing on real returns, and avoid exposure to sequence of returns. You can get there by being tactical in your investing style. Tactical is a sailing term used when you are sailing against the wind. You need to be tactical to go side by side, tacking back and forth so you can go up wind.

Investing goals should not be to try to beat an index every year. Your goal should be to beat it over a full market cycle. You need to navigate the upside of the market and the downside of the market. Remember those 22 prior major market corrections averaging a loss of 37%? The goal should be to capture 70%-80% of the market cycle upside while only participating in 10%-20% of the downside of the market cycle while keeping your losses to under 10%.

All investing goals should be to get the most return while suffering the least amount of losses after all fees and expenses. If you do this you should keep up with the market upsides and minimize your downside exposure.

By being tactical you focus on minimizing your losses so you can stay ahead in the long run. Being tactical is also like being the tortoise in the race against the hare. You remember who wins that race.

When you invest tactically you increase the possibility of living your five-year increments without the waiting game of getting back to even.

The following illustration shows how tactical management works.

You would sell after the market starts to show signs of weakness and re-enter the market after there are signs of strength. As you can see you will never capture 100% of the upside of the market and you will not participate in 100% of the downside of the market or losses.

Tactical Investing Chart

We believe building a portfolio of tactical strategies will minimize your downside risk in retirement allowing you to keep focused on maintaining your lifestyle.

How Tactical Asset Management Works

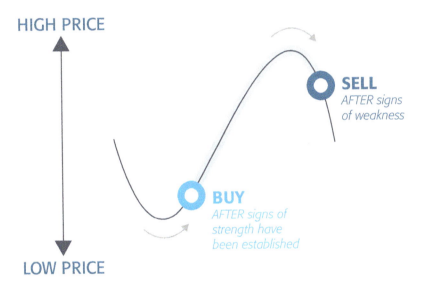

CHAPTER 12
THE IMPORTANCE OF MINIMIZING LOSSES

When planning investment returns, you should have a plan to minimize your losses. We have been taught our investing life that if we get 6%, 7% or 8% average returns we will be ok. During retirement and leading up to retirement we need to be thinking a little different. How much am I willing to lose to get the 6%, 7% or 8% return? On average when the stock market has its major falls it takes five to six years to get back to even.

The chart on the next page illustrates how much it takes just to get back to even when you lose money. Southerners have a saying that "the farther you fall into a ditch the harder it is to climb out." In other words "the larger the loss, the larger the gain needs to be just to make your money back." Losses impact the amount of money you have remaining to spend and could impact your ability to live your five-year life increment plan.

The Math of Recovery From a Portfolio Loss

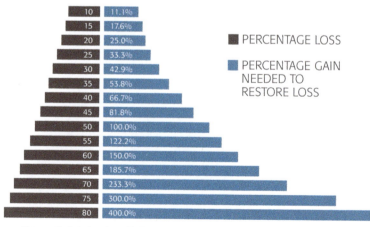

Source: Craig L. Israelsen, Ph.D

Going forward, start thinking in terms of dollars and not average losses. Let's use an example with money. Let's start with $100,000. If you lose 30% you now have $70,000. It is common belief that it only takes 30% to get to even. Well, a 30% gain on $70,000 is only $91,000. You are still shy by $9,000. It actually takes a 43% gain to get back to $100,000.

If you had an advisor during 2009 during the start of the last recovery, you probably heard "we made 29% this year." What they should have told you is "we recovered 29% of your losses." We call this recovering old money.

Take the total amount of money you have saved and ask yourself: In retirement am I ok with suffering through a 20% to 30% loss? On $1,000,000 that is a $200,000 to $300,000 loss. On $500,000 that is a $100,000 to $150,000 loss. Compare that to how much you paid for your first home. Or how long it took you to save your first $100,000. By knowing it takes on average six years to get back to even, how much of a loss are you willing to suffer during retirement?

We see it time and time again that when people lose money they put off or never take their big bucket list trip. We think big losses impact a couple's ability to focus on maintaining their five-year lifestyle.

In retirement, you should be focusing on investments that have either no risk of loss or strategies that will minimize your losses. We will talk about this in more detail in later chapters.

CHAPTER 13
UNDERSTANDING THE TRUE MEANING OF RETURNS "REAL VS. AVERAGE"

"The day you retire, average returns no longer apply."
Tom Henga, former First Vice President at New York Life

This is the most misunderstood concept that most financial professionals miss during the planning process. We like to say this is a missing critical fact that can mislead people into a false sense of confidence in planning. Most financial planning software programs will ask you what is the average return you are expecting during your retirement. Sounds like a simple answer. We hear it all the time. A 5%-7% average return should get me to enjoy a happy retirement.

We want to address something that is so important in retirement planning. Average returns can be misleading. We want you to start focusing on real returns and not average returns. What is the difference? Let's use some simple math.

Year 1: you gain 50%

Year 2: you lose 50%

What is the average return? Not a trick question. The average return is 0%.

You would think everything is ok with that since you didn't lose any money. The problem is that it is a common misconception. Now let's put the same example to money.

Start with $1,000. Year 1 you made 50%. You now have $1,500. Year 2 you lose 50%. You now have $750. That is a negative 25% real rate of return, not a 0% return.

Plug in a 0% return in that online planning software and it can say you will be ok. What you thought was a good plan isn't a good plan if you lost money in the market.

Now when would you have wanted to know this fact about averages? Before you made a decision to retire, or 5 to 10 years into retirement?

Ok that was a simple example. Let's do this with another example comparing returns of two accounts.

Which account would you pick?

Account A:	
YEAR 1	+5%
YEAR 2	+5%
YEAR 3	+5%
Average return 5%	

Account B:	
YEAR 1	+30%
YEAR 2	-20%
YEAR 3	+5%
Average return 5%	

Account A: $100,000		
YR 1	+5%	$105,000
YR 2	+5%	$110,250
YR 3	+5%	$115,762.50
Average return 5%		

Account B: $100,000		
YR 1	+30%	$130,000
YR 2	-20%	$104,000
YR 3	+5%	$109,200
Average return 5%		

They both have the same average of 5%. Even if you change the return order you will still get the same average. (Make the first year lose 20%, the second year gain 5% and then gain 30% in the third year. Still a 5% average return.)

These two accounts can legally advertise to you, that their account averaged a 5% return. Now let's put real money to the accounts and start each account with $100,000. Still know which one you want to pick?

After year 1 the person with account B at the dinner party was bragging to their friends that their advisor got them 30%. After year 2 the person with account B was no longer bragging because they lost 20% of their money. After the third year who was bragging about their account? The tortoise or the hare?

When you do the math, a $9,200 gain is 9.2% and the three-year real or actual rate of return is roughly 3.1%, much less than the misleading 5% average return most investors look at. How would your plan work if you used a 5% average in your projections, but only got a 3% real return? It is important to work with a planner that understands this. The reason for the difference is when you have a loss in any series of years, then the average return will always be higher than what the real return will provide you.

Remember the opening quote in this chapter. It is true because you cannot spend average returns you can only spend actual returns.

Remember what we talked about in the chapter about the importance of minimizing losses.

CHAPTER 14
SEQUENCE OF RETURN RISK

It's not about what the returns are but when the returns happen.

We have found that most people do not understand what "Sequence of Returns" risk actually is. Before Brian got involved in retirement planning his father experienced a bad sequence of returns but didn't realize what was happening until a year or two later after he retired.

His father retired early as an engineering manager at the early age of 55 in 1999. He read lots of financial magazines, read the business section of the newspaper daily and listened to his co-worker's strategies. He and Brian's mom sacrificed some things and did an excellent job at savings so they could retire early. His Income plan was simple. Withdraw from his savings for seven years and start Social Security at 62. He put a conservative return at the time of 7% on his investments. Well everything was working just fine until a year later in 2000. The technology bubble started to burst. He had been investing in technology and other stock funds because he was young and could handle some risk.

He had learned that if he pulled 4% from his savings and earned 4% then he would be ok in retirement. Well, what happened was he started pulling his 4% to meet his spending needs. What he didn't know was that as the market was falling, his 4% turned into 5% then 6% then 8% quickly even with him pulling the same amount that was his original starting withdrawal amount.

In 2001 Brian's father told him that he thought he would have to go back to work if the market didn't turn around and make him money again. Brian said, "Dad, you did an excellent job saving and you should be ok, right?" He then told Brian, "Either I go back to work or someday your mother and I will have to move in with you." Can you imagine the stress and anxiety that Brian's parents must have felt? And the stress and anxiety on Brian.

What happened to Brian's father was the impact of when those losses occurred. If the market would have grown shortly after he retired versus having losses, he would have been better off.

You see it only matters on when you pull money out when you have losses. If you don't need to spend the money, then losses have a smaller impact on retirement. The problem is that as we age we don't have much time left to recover those losses so keeping the losses to a minimum is important.

The following page is an example of pulling money out and having losses versus gains when you retire.

Both Investors are age 65.

Both start with $500,000.

Both portfolios average a 6% net return.

Both withdraw 5% over 30 years. Both investors need the $25,000 to cover the shortfall of income.

Investor A – poor returns earlier and stronger return later

Investor B – positive returns earlier and poor returns later

Investor A depleted their assets in year 16 around age 81.

Investor B did not run out of money.

THE SEQUENCE OF RETURNS

INVESTOR A – EARLY LOSS

YEAR	S&P 500 INDEX ANNUAL TOTAL RETURN	$500,000	AMOUNT WITHDRAWN
2000	-9.10%	$429,500.00	$25,000
2001	-11.89%	$352,682.45	$25,750
2002	-22.10%	$248,217.13	$26,523
2003	28.68%	$292,087.63	$27,318
2004	10.88%	$295,729.04	$28,138
2005	4.91%	$281,267.48	$28,982
2006	15.79%	$295,828.31	$29,851
2007	5.49%	$281,322.44	$30,747
2008	-37.00%	$145,563.88	$31,669
2009	26.46%	$151,460.76	$32,619
2010	15.06%	$140,672.84	$33,598
2011	2.11%	$109,035.19	$34,606
2012	16.00%	$90,836.80	$35,644
2013	32.39%	$83,545.49	$36,713
2014	13.69%	$57,168.13	$37,815
2015	1.38%	$19,007.86	$38,949
2016	11.96%	**$(18,836.46)**	$40,118
AVERAGE RATE OF RETURN	**6.2%**		**$544,040**

INVESTOR B – EARLY GAIN

YEAR	S&P 500 INDEX ANNUAL TOTAL RETURN	$500,000	AMOUNT WITHDRAWN
2016	11.96%	$534,800.00	$25,000
2015	1.38%	$516,430.24	$25,750
2014	13.69%	$560,607.04	$26,523
2013	32.39%	$714,869.49	$27,318
2012	16.00%	$801,110.88	$28,138
2011	2.11%	$789,032.47	$28,982
2010	15.06%	$878,009.45	$29,851
2009	26.46%	$1,079,583.91	$30,747
2008	-37.00%	$648,468.61	$31,669
2007	5.49%	$651,450.21	$32,619
2006	15.79%	$720,716.28	$33,598
2005	4.91%	$721,497.61	$34,606
2004	10.88%	$764,352.53	$35,644
2003	28.68%	$946,855.49	$36,713
2002	-22.10%	$699,785.68	$37,815
2001	-11.89%	$577,631.98	$38,949
2000	-9.10%	**$484,949.81**	$40,118
AVERAGE RATE OF RETURN	**6.2%**		**$544,040**

AMOUNT WITHDRAWN ASSUMES 5% ANNUAL WITHDRAWALS OF $25,000 INCREASING AT 3% ANNUALLY FOR INFLATION.

Drop the withdrawal rate to 3% then the probability of everything working out correct increased to 84%.

That's like taking an airplane on a trip and the pilot says, "Welcome aboard, the weather will be 85 and sunny and we have a 64% chance of getting to our destination." Would you still stay on that plane? Be careful about using general advice in your planning process.

Sequence of return risk applies to you even if you do not need to pull money from your retirement assets for income. At 70½ you need to take your required minimum distributions (RMDS) out of your tax-deferred retirement accounts. If all your expenses are covered by pensions and Social Security and maybe rental income this can happen to you. If your IRAs drop in value and you pull out those RMDs your account will be subject to the risk and struggle to get back to even. Even if you pay your taxes on the RMDs and reinvest it you still have less money and it is hard to recover the losses.

You wonder what Brian's dad did? He went back to work for a couple of years to stop the bleeding in his investment accounts and then re-retired again at 62 in 2006. This allowed his investments to recover some of the losses and for Brian's dad to start claiming Social Security. What happened just one year later in October 2007? Look at the bear market chart in the market cycles chapter. That's right. The start of the largest market correction since the Great Depression. Can you imagine the stress and anxiety his parents were feeling? The phrase "Oh No, here we go again," comes to mind. The good news is that their pensions and Social Security benefits covered most of their expenses on a guaranteed basis. We covered this in the income chapter.

CHAPTER 15
HEALTHCARE

None of us want to be unhealthy. But we do need to plan for the time that we may not be in the best of health. Healthcare costs come in many forms. Premiums for Medicare. Out-of-pocket expenses like co-pays and deductibles for doctors and prescriptions. And, ultimately, the cost of potential long-term care needs.

We do know that premiums have kept increasing over the last decade. So with proper planning, we suggest you take the cost of care and increase that each year by 6% above the inflation rate. We suggest using an inflation rate of 3%. Increase healthcare costs, including premiums, by at least 9% each year.

We need to look at healthcare in two parts. First, after 65 most of us will be on a Medicare plan. Second, we need to consider our healthcare choices before 65 and what to do if we still plan on working beyond 65.

In considering our healthcare choices before we reach 65 we need to look at options that may be available. If you happen to be one of the people caught up in layoffs before the age of 65 there are a couple choices available to you. Currently, if your old company is around then you have the option of COBRA[10] coverage. This coverage allows you and your dependents to continue for 18 months on your old employer's plan. If you happen to be a widow or widower then you can elect to have COBRA coverage for up to 36 months. There are time restrictions for siging up through COBRA, so don't delay if you are eligible.

There are also private insurance options as well. Shop around as coverages, premiums, deductables and co-pays vary by plan. Pick one that works well with your plan. If you are married then you may have the option of going on your spouse's plan until it is time to go on Medicare. We do know that premiums are typically higher than you are used to paying but don't let this discourage you from retiring early if your income and investment plan works.

As for Medicare most every one will need to sign up at age 65 unless you plan on working for an employer that has more than 20 employees. If you do then you won't have to sign up until you coverage ends. You may also want to work with a Medicare broker to review your corporate plan versus the coverages available on Medicare. Sometimes you can get better coverage for less premiums than your employer plan offers.

For one, we do recommend that everyone use the services of a Medicare broker that is licensed with all the companies that can do business in the state they reside in. Medicare brokers can do all the leg work for you and continue to look for the best plans available to you each year. They do get the same exact premiums that you can get if you were to take the time yourself to shop and compare coverages directly with the insurance companies. They will help navigate the many different options for you without charging for their services. They get paid from the insurance companies much like your home and auto insurance agents. The thing we like about the good Medicare brokers is that they are required to stay up on all changes each year. Consider working with a broker about six months before you turn 65.

Medicare.gov is a great resource for information on Medicare choices. We will be brief in our descriptions and going to the website for more clarifying information is important. As planners, we want you to be aware of the costs and choices you will have to make.

There are four main parts to Medicare.

Part A covers hospitals.

Part B covers the doctors, procedures, and preventative services.

Part C covers Parts A and B and usually Part D. Think of this as your traditional HMO[11] or PPO[12] type services.

Part D covers prescription drugs.

Another thing to consider in retirement is your prescription coverages and the costs. As explained earlier Medicare Part D covers prescription drugs. There are several plans available so it is important to shop the plans around each year as the prescription drugs you take may change tiers and you might have to pay more out-of-pocket for that.

It is important to enroll on time or you will be subject to penalties on your Part B and Part D premiums for the rest of your retirement. The penalties for missing your Part B enrollment period is 10% for each year you miss signing up. For Part D it is a penalty of 1% per month for not signing up on time (within 63 days of when you were supposed to).

To avoid penalties and gaps of coverage there is a seven-month window to sign up for Medicare. For most people, you can sign up for Medicare three months before the month you turn 65 to have Medicare start when you are 65. The month you turn 65 (coverage started the next month) and three months after your 65th birthday. This will allow you to avoid penalties. However, you will have a month or two of no coverage if you sign up in the three months after your 65th birthday.

If you are working past the age of 65 and your employer has 20 or more employees then you can sign up for Medicare after your coverage ends. Technically you have up to eight months after your coverage ends for Medicare but only 63 days to file for Medicare Part D to avoid the penalties. You will have a gap in coverage and you do not want to get sick if you have no coverage.

Now if you have a lot of income you may also be subject to an income-related adjustment called the Medicare surcharge tax on your Part B and Part D premiums. This is a two-year look back period and the surcharge tax is only charged one year at a time. Please refer to the Medicare.gov website for the current surcharges as the government has been lowering the income tiers. This is done so that higher income earners pay more for Medicare to help balance out the benefits among all participants. Medicare surcharges are calculated using your AGI plus any tax-exempt interest. Be careful here as you may not originally have to pay the extra premium tax but can be pushed into this by receiving an inheritance, the passing of a spouse and/or your required minimum distributions. We will cover this more in the tax chapters of the book.

Because everyone must make this choice in retirement and there are so many moving parts we remind you that working with knowledgeable advisors is important.

CHAPTER 16
HAVE A LONG-TERM CARE PLAN

Do you have a long-term care plan? Did you notice that we didn't ask if you had long- term care insurance? There are several ways to plan for long-term care (LTC). The fact that we Americans are living longer today makes it a multiplier that we may need to have some sort of long-term care services. When we look at a long-term care plan we look at it as an "anti-nursing home care plan." Today, most care for long-term care starts out in the individual's residence and increases to skilled nursing as the level of care needed progresses. Let's face it. None of us wants to be unhealthy enough to need to go into a home.

There are several ways to address long-term care. Traditional long-term care insurance; newer short-term insurance coverage (12 months of coverage); life insurance that allows a person to use the death benefit during their lifetime for long-term care; fixed annuities that allow for long-term care coverage; fixed-indexed annuities that allow for income riders to increase the income if there is a need for long-term care; the use of your savings to cover any cost of care; and, last but not least, we can always rely on our family members to take time off work to care for us when we need the care.

The issue with long-term care is there is a cost for the care. Remember there is a cost to do something and a cost to do nothing. We are living longer and our longevity will act as a multiplier that increases the chance that we will be unhealthy and need medical care. Depending on the amount of care and diagnosis it will impact the surviving spouse and potentially impact their quality of life after the first person passes away.

We want to tell a quick story as to why you should address long-term care with some sort of long-term care solution. Brian was traveling back to California in 2015 to visit his family for Christmas, a couple weeks after the passing of his mother. On the way back to Colorado he ran into an old employee of his from the past. His family also lives in California and his father was diagnosed with Alzheimer's. In talking, Brian learned that he was flying back every other week and trading weeks with his brother to help their mother with their father. They had been doing that for eight months prior to Christmas. Brian asked if they had any long-term care insurance on his father. He said funny thing you ask Brian. He told Brian that they bought long-term care insurance over 10 years ago and his father wanted to stop it because the premiums were getting expensive. He had convinced his father to keep paying it because you never know. They did and it took seven months to convince his mother to use the policy to bring in outside help. They were married for 53 years and she had a tough time of not wanting to care for her husband. Help finally came in to relieve their mother and both sons. They currently are spending about $500 a day for round-the-clock care in the house. The family was relieved that they had the insurance because they were not sure how long he would be living with Alzheimer's and requiring this level of care. Without the coverage, they would be spending around $15,000 each month which would leave their mother with not much left if he lived another four or five years.

Long-term care takes its toll on the caregiver which usually starts out with the spouse or a family member. It also can take a toll on the surviving spouse by having a chance to deplete the remaining assets. Considering some coverage is usually better than no coverage at all.

In covering the costs of care and coverage it is important to look at the income sources that can be used to help offset the cost of care. Social Security and pensions will continue to be received while you or your spouse needs care. As a minimum, you want to bridge the cost of care with the income coming in. Covering the difference can be a good idea as well as looking at ways to preserve assets for your surviving spouse.

A common misconception is people think that Medicare covers LTC. Medicare can cover some care if the patient has a chance to recover but the coverage is minimal. Medicaid does cover LTC costs for those with little to no assets. In Colorado, you can have a home, one car and $2,000 in cash and investments. The rules do vary by state so we suggest you check with your state. We are not proponents of using strategies to minimize your assets to qualify for Medicaid. You generally will limit your care choices and there is a five-year look-back period just to qualify.

Ask yourself, "What is your LTC plan?"

CHAPTER 17
TAX-EFFICIENCY PLANNING

Any one may so arrange his affairs that his taxes shall be as low as possible; he is not bound to choose that pattern which will best pay the Treasury; there is not even a patriotic duty to increase one's taxes.
— Judge Learned Hand[13]

Judge Learned Hand says it best and is one of the most quoted judges in the tax court. We agree that all of us should pay our fair share in taxes. However, there is no reason to pay more than necessary. We spend our working careers looking for ways to reduce our income taxes. Many people don't think much about how to lower taxes throughout retirement. Do you know what surveys each year for those retired five years or more find on what the biggest surprise is that people have in retirement? It is taxes.

Remember when you started saving in your company's 401(k)? What was the thing they told you when you contributed? They told you contribute today and get a tax deduction on your income today and when you retire you will be in a lower tax bracket.

For those who have a lot of their income saved from pensions and Social Security, their largest annual expense in retirement is taxes. Most people just look to see what they owe or what their refund will be when they complete their taxes instead of looking at what the total tax for the year was. Pull out last year's taxes and look at the total tax on page 2. Is it more than your annual mortgage or rent payments? More than your vacation spending? Car payments?

If it is, then you should consider working with your advisor, CPA and tax attorney to be as tax efficient as possible. The best tax bracket in retirement is the 0% tax bracket.

Did you know that taxes are entirely voluntary? For most people, they are involuntary as they aren't aware of the more than 100 opportunities within the IRS tax code. Most people look at the restrictions the tax code has versus the opportunities that lie within the code to be tax free. Working with CPAs and tax attorneys is a must to put together a good tax plan.

There are three ways investments and income are taxed.

Taxable – Investments are taxed as they are earned each year.

Tax Deferred – Investments that, for a deduction taken today, will be taxed when withdrawn. This also creates compound interest. It also creates a compounding tax problem as well.

Tax Free – Investments grow tax deferred and are tax free when withdrawn.

Common accounts found in each are as follows:

Taxable – checking, savings, CDs, brokerage investment accounts;

Tax Deferred – 401(k)s, traditional IRAs, SEP and simple IRAs, 403(b), 401(a)s, 457s; and

Tax Free – Roth IRAs, Roth 401(k)s, cash value of permanent life insurance.

We look at the three different taxes as the tax triangle.

TAX TRIANGLE

There is a proper balance under the tax code to get to a 0% tax bracket and it is extremely rare that people are even close to that. What we see is that people are heavy in the tax-deferred portion and this causes them to be in higher tax brackets and not tax efficient at all. The main reason for this is that the IRS has an income plan for all your tax-deferred monies. We say that the IRS has a mortgage on your IRA and 401(k)s. It is called required minimum distributions (RMDs). At 70½ you must start paying the mortgage back to the IRS on your accounts by pulling money from your tax-deferred accounts or there is a penalty. Be careful not to miss this as of the writing of this book it is a 50% penalty on the amount you were supposed to withdraw.

We believe that it is extremely important to be as tax efficient as possible to minimize or eliminate the amount of taxes you will pay throughout the rest of your life. Has anyone shown you how to minimize or eliminate the taxes you pay on your tax-deferred accounts? Has anyone shown you ways to minimize or eliminate taxes during retirement?

What we find is that most tax accountants or CPAs are typically historians. They look at what you did last year and try to minimize what you pay in income taxes for the prior year. And most financial advisors focus on investments with minimal consideration to taxation. When was the last time your accountant or CPA came to you and said let me show you ways to eliminate your future taxes?

To be tax efficient requires much thought and strategy to meet the goals of the individual or couples. Tax-efficiency planning needs to be addressed and looked at in two ways. One, taxes paid during your lifetime and two, taxes that occur when your assets pass to your children and grandchildren upon your death. We are not talking of estate taxes but the income taxes on your assets. You can be extremely efficient during your lifetime but have your assets subject to even more taxation upon your death.

Generally, there are three ways future taxation could be. Taxes could stay the same, go up, or down. What we find is that most people think that taxes will be going up. This belief stems from the current government deficit spending, the lowest top end marginal tax rate in history, and a need to fund the overall government over time. We are in the camp that taxes will go up. Most people ignore the statistics but the Congressional Budget Office that provides Congress with budget and economic information, states the biggest line item of our U.S. government in 2027 will be the interest on our debt. We won't bore you with the details but they can be found at CBO. gov. It comes down to one simple word in the dictionary. The word is math. The math tells us that we need either growth of the U.S. economy, an increase in taxes, or a combination of both.

Always remember this. There is always a cost to do something and there is always a cost to do nothing.

Here are ways to be tax efficient. We recommend that you work with professional advisors that understand these as well as your current tax advisor.

You can invest your non-IRA monies in municipal bonds which allows for the interest to be tax free on the federal level, and tax free on the state level if it is a municipal bond of a municipality of the state you live in. Be careful here because capital gains and distributions are taxable each year. Only the interest can be tax free.

Did you know that capital gains taxes, estate taxes and income taxes from your tax-deferred accounts are entirely voluntary? If you have a proper plan then you can minimize or eliminate these taxes.

Have a retirement income plan to keep your annual income in the lowest tax bracket possible. This requires you to spend from all parts of the tax triangle. Although this could be good during your lifetime it could cause more income taxes when you die.

Consider the multiple exit strategies from your tax-deferred accounts. These strategies if properly designed and executed can minimize and/or eliminate taxation on your withdrawals.

Roth conversions are the most common strategy. However, if not properly executed they can result in you paying more income tax as well as subjecting you to the Medicare surcharge tax as well as taxes on your Social Security payments.

Synthetic Roth conversions using a permanent life insurance policy. This can create leveraged up monies that transfer to the next generation tax free as well as create tax-free income using the cash value within the policies. Be careful here as the policy needs to be designed properly and many advisors do not know how to design them correctly.

Using charitable planning in a strategic plan to not only benefit the charity but also yourself. There are several strategies you can deploy to help many people. Of course, you can be very charitable and have the IRS be the biggest charity you donate to. OK, here is how the IRS is a charity. You pay to the IRS and they distribute to many social programs that help the American people. It's just you can't control how they spend your tax dollars.

If you are a business owner there are several strategies to sell your business and not be subject to the gains tax from the sale.

If you own rental properties what is your tax exit strategy to sell them and minimize or eliminate the taxes paid?

With over 72,000 pages of the IRS tax code it is important to use strategies that work within the tax code. We do not recommend avoiding paying taxes but use strategies that are allowed within the tax code to your advantage, not only during your lifetime, but also when you pass your hard-earned money to the next generations.

CHAPTER 18
CHARITABLE AND PHILANTHROPIC PLANNING

Do you participate in voluntary or involuntary charitable giving? When we ask this question we always get answers like this: we like to give to our church, social welfare programs like the United Way, American Cancer Society, or the local food bank or homeless programs and many others too long to list. We love hearing the stories of what motivates them to do so.

We also love charitable giving because it is our opportunity to give back to our community and society and we list the charities we support on our website apofinancial.com.

Most of the time people would like to donate more than they have in the past but don't because they are concerned about giving away too much money as it may hurt their income plan.

We have found that all Americans are involuntary philanthropists. When we point this out in our meetings people don't quite understand this statement. When we show people that they are very good givers. They just happen to give to the largest charity each year in the United States. That charity is called the IRS. We touched on this in the prior chapter on taxes.

When you think about it the IRS collects our taxes and distributes it the way they see fit without our input on where our money goes. We always say if you don't want to pay for that $400 toilet seat or hammer then look for ways to minimize your taxes.

There are over a half dozen strategies available to reposition assets while maintaining control of your money and income to increase your voluntary philanthropic goals while minimizing or eliminating your current and future involuntary tax donations.

Sounds crazy but there are over 100 opportunities within the

72,000 pages of the IRS tax code to minimize and or eliminate your taxes. If you do it right the IRS may even give you a credit or tax deduction for doing it correctly. You need to work with advisors that understand these and make a change and/or addition if you have outgrown your current advisors' capabilities.

This area of planning shouldn't be going down a road of doing it all by yourself. As the tax code is ever changing you need to work with CPAs and tax attorneys that specialize in the charitable area of planning and keep up with the changes.

Even though we have experience in this area we often bring in out of town experts who specialize in this area. They will analyze all the options available and find out which option or options align with your goals and desires before recommending the solution. With proper planning, you can eliminate the IRS from being your largest beneficiary when you die.

CHAPTER 19
FINANCIAL ESTATE PLANNING

Oh, the topic no one wants to address. We had a client tell us once that I don't want to do an estate plan because it makes me realize that I will die someday. Talk about putting a head in the sand. We like to think of this part of the planning process as estate preparation. If you don't prepare properly you can expose your children to additional income taxes, infighting if your wishes are not clear and delays in getting your assets to the proper people.

We approach estate planning based on another conversation we had with a client early in our practice. They phrased it this way. "We want to create a legacy plan based on our values so our future generations can not only benefit from our money but by our examples." Another way of saying this is that you can create a legacy of values that can last over many generations.

We have found that many people want to have an estate plan but think that estate plans are just for the wealthy. They also believe that it costs a lot of money to put one together. We believe that everyone should have an estate plan. It comes in many shapes and forms from a basic will to a full plan with multiple trusts. What we see is that most plans are set up to avoid the headaches of the probate process which it does. But it doesn't solve all the financial questions of taxes and how your money is spent and the wishes you had for your money.

We call the process financial estate planning which takes into consideration a lot more detail than just passing money outside of probate. There is above the line planning and below the line planning. Ask yourself what type of life print do you want to leave behind?

Everyone should have at least the basic estate plan that includes a will and, both medical and financial directives commonly known as "powers of attorney." We call this above the line planning. The basic plan makes everything about you when you pass public knowledge.

In other words, it is not that you have passed on, but the amounts you have are now known to everyone. Think about the phone calls to your children asking them to invest in this and that. The get rich quick schemes come out of the woodwork. When we review current plans, often times the plans only focus on getting the money to the right people or places like charitable organizations.

Below the line planning focuses on getting the right amount to the right people and organizations at the right time. This planning allows you to set up revocable trusts to pass the money on to your children and grandchildren. By setting up trusts this keeps the amount you have private so that the world isn't aware of what your beneficiaries have received.

When creating your legacy plan, you can take a few steps to further control what happens, ranging from the amount of taxes paid to how your money is spent. When passing money to your children and grandchildren you can protect your hard-earned money from future estate taxes, judgements, creditors and liens, and assets counted in a bankruptcy. Another one we see is that people want protection from their children's future ex-spouses. This involves a series of irrevocable trusts (meaning the trusts can't be changed). They are also called Dynasty or Heritage trusts.

We bring this up because, through the many conversations we have with people, they often say our children or grandchildren don't spend money like we do. Or that they don't like their children's spouses or partners. Or the future spouses of your children or grandchildren.

Another part of financial estate planning is an annual review of your beneficiaries on your IRAs and 401(k)s. We see it time and time again that ex-spouses or deceased spouses are listed when they shouldn't be. Many times a child has been left off inadvertently.

We caution you to fall into the belief that our children are doing well because they have a good education and jobs. Sometimes we often believe that our children have good paying jobs and that they are or will always be doing well.

We had a client list all three children on the IRAs she had with us.

We advised her to change her beneficiaries on her work 401(k) because only two of her three children were listed. She said the one left off was a lawyer and doing well and that she was trying to help the other two children who had her grandkids.

Over time the lawyer child got married and had two children. Well after having their own children they weren't as well off but they didn't talk about money as a family. When she passed, there was some animosity and hurt feeling as the lawyer child felt left out because he wasn't part of that portion of asset distribution. The good news is the other two siblings brought the other one even. We point this out because there is no legal obligation for the other two children to have done that.

People that have no children or grandchildren should also have a plan. You can make sure money or property goes to other family members or charities. There are many options that can help so many people through charitable giving, foundation planning, scholarships, or even creating grants for nonprofit organizations.

One of our favorite stories is a doctor who wanted to help create scholarships for other children who grew up with a single parent. They wanted to list as beneficiary their alma mater. We were able to show her a way to set up scholarships before she passed away so she could see some of the people she is helping while she is alive.

Figuring out your wishes should be thought through with many factors to take into consideration. Work with an advisor and team who can help guide you through the decisions as well as guide you to the proper legal professionals to have your wishes honored.

CHAPTER 20
FIND YOUR LIFE PRINT

Do you remember your great grandparents' first names? After all they are the reason you are here.

We find that going through the process of planning allows people to take as much of the stress and anxiety out of retirement as possible. By doing so and focusing on the suggestions and information we laid out in the prior chapters you will develop a plan to leave your life print.

When we say this is what do you want to be remembered for? Do you want your great grandchildren to remember your first name? What is your bigger impact that you want to leave for your children?

We like to take our clients through what we call a mind mapping process that allows them to start thinking about the life print that they would like to leave. This process allows our clients to get more money to their families and private charities and less or none to the IRS. Our goal is focus on your bigger impact and looking for ways to achieve that.

Going through a complete planning process allows you to Smile Through Retirement and have a clearer picture of your path and journey to living your life in five-year increments and ultimately leaving your life print on the future generations to come.

ABOUT THE AUTHORS

Both Brian and Ray have articles published on Fortune.com, Money.com, cnnmoney.com, and foxbusiness.com.

They are known as nationally recognized financial educators, authors, speakers, radio hosts and retirement planners, whom you may have seen on NBC, ABC, CBS, and FOX network affiliates, and Bloomberg Business, Yahoo Finance, Investing Daily, Wall Street Select, MarketWatch, and others.

They co-created the Smiling Through Retirement Process™ out of a passion to help people plan their retirement with a focus on living it as they dreamed it.

They were hosts of a radio show called Stepping into Retirement on the weekends in Denver on 630 AM.

They are also featured several times a year taking live call-in questions on the Tom Martino Troubleshooter show.

BRIAN GRAY

Brian is a fiduciary advisor and a founder of APO Financial in Colorado. He has clients throughout the U.S. Brian was born and raised in Southern California and has been a Colorado resident since 2002. He has a Finance degree from California State University of Fullerton. He resides in Arapahoe County with his long-term girlfriend and life partner Ashley. They love to travel, scuba dive, golf and watch live music. Brian and Ashley are believers in the five-year increments and do fulfill their bucket list items.

RAY STEIN

Ray is a native of Colorado and resides in Douglass County with his wife Arisa and son. He earned his Finance degree from the University of Colorado and got his financial start in the high-risk world of option, stock, futures and currency trading. He became a fiduciary advisor and has been with APO Financial since 2013. Ray and his family love to travel, spend time with family, volunteer at church and various charitable organizations.

YOUR NEXT STEPS

Now that you have read the book it is important to put the information you learned to use. The best thing to do is reach out to the APO team to review your personal situation to make sure you are on the right path to smile through retirement.

CONTACT THEM AT

Brian@apofinancial.com

Ray@apofinancial.com

Office line: 720-588-2000

VIDEOS:
www.youtube.com/channel/UCPB-_SDmm6VJoVgNkiQSjeQ youtube/apofinancial

WEBSITE:
Apofinancial.com

BLOGS:
APOfinancial.com/blogs

If you are nearing retirement you need to watch out for planning based on general rules. The amount of retirement advice found on the "How to retire" search on Google leads to 5.9 million pages on the subject.

This book will help you sort through the common advice that can steer you in the wrong direction. It is much better to know that you are on the right path.

The authors are featured on Fortune, Money, CNN Money, and Fox Business. You may have seen them on NBC, ABC, CBS, Yahoo Finance, Investing Daily, Wall Street Select, MarketWatch and others.

"If you want to understand the importance of planning for your retirement or you are already retired you must read Smiling Through Retirement." It is simple, engaging, thought provoking and will put you on the right path to enjoy your retirement to the fullest. Do not let the little things that most people don't see have an effect in the five key areas of retirement planning that you will learn. Want to have the retirement you desire? This book is a must read."

– ERIC SCOTT, 2015 Advisor of the Year - Retirement Advisor Magazine

---

SOURCES

[1] http://www.cancerresearchuk.org/health-professional/cancer-statistics/incidence/age

[2] https://www.ssa.gov/history/taxationofbenefits.html

[3] https://www.ssa.gov/policy/docs/issuepapers/ip2015-02.html

[4] (The Social Security Dilemma)

[5] (National Center for Health Statistics, 2017)

[6] "Managing Retirement Risks- A Guide to Retirement Planning" Society of Actuaries Oct. 2011 Web. 26 Mar. 2014

[7] "Historic inflation United States - CPI inflation" Inflation.eu 2017 Web. Mar. 2017

[8] https://www.forbes.com/sites/feeonlyplanner/2012/07/02/9-reasons-you-need-to-avoid-variable-annuities/#4bce0d465f19

[9] Investment grade life insurance companies are generally rate Baa3 or higher by Moody's Investors Service or BBB- or higher as rated by Standard & Poor's and Fitch Ratings. Insurer financial strength ratings of B+ and above are considered Secure by A.M. Best.

[10] The Consolidated Omnibus Budget Reconciliation Act

[11] Health Maintenance Organization

[12] Preferred Provider Organization

[13] Gregory v. Helvering, 69 F.2d 809, 810 (2d Cir. 1934)

CPSIA information can be obtained
at www.ICGtesting.com
Printed in the USA
BVHW092104211019
561717BV00004B/12/P